T0156983

10 TRUTHS®
OF SONGWRITING

10 TRUTHS®
OF SONGWRITING

A SURVIVAL GUIDE

CHRIS M. WILL

10 TRUTHS® OF SONGWRITING
A SURVIVAL GUIDE

iUniverse books may be ordered through booksellers or by contacting:

iUniverse
1663 Liberty Drive
Bloomington, IN 47403
www.iuniverse.com
1-800-Authors (1-800-288-4677)

Because of the dynamic nature of the Internet, any web addresses or links contained in this book may have changed since publication and may no longer be valid. The views expressed in this work are solely those of the author and do not necessarily reflect the views of the publisher, and the publisher hereby disclaims any responsibility for them.

Any people depicted in stock imagery provided by Thinkstock are models, and such images are being used for illustrative purposes only. Certain stock imagery © Thinkstock.

ISBN: 978-1-4917-7449-6 (sc)
ISBN: 978-1-4917-7532-5 (e)

Library of Congress Control Number: 2015913347

Print information available on the last page.

iUniverse rev. date: 08/26/2015

Contents

Introduction

I have been a music person my whole life—starting from the time I was three years old growing up in suburban Cincinnati. My earliest musical memory is my pretending to play piano while singing along with "Lookin' Out My Back Door" by Creedence Clearwater Revival. I'm not sure why I was pretending to play piano, because there's no piano in the song, but music put its hooks into my soul at an early age. I'm confident that it had something to do with my father, who loved music and used to play his Johnny Cash and Elvis Presley records all the time. He would also pull out his acoustic guitar to play "Folsom Prison Blues" from time to time. My brother was grabbed by music early too, so he was probably the other major influence. I recently uncovered some eight-millimeter video of him playing drums and me playing guitar at Christmas. The video had no sound, but I'm sure it was, at best, a lot of noise.

I was about six the first time my father let us try his electric guitar and amp. I dropped the guitar, breaking the cord jack. I don't think my dad ever got that jack fixed, and we never tried again. But we always had acoustic guitars around the house to mess with.

My brother got heavily into music in the 1970s. He was learning to play guitar and taking lessons. Being four years older than I, he dragged me along for the ride. As the younger brother, I always wanted to do whatever he did. So by 1975, at the age of seven, I was into rock and roll big-time. I was a huge fan of Aerosmith and Led Zeppelin, and then I saw the Kiss *Alive* album at Kmart.

Of course my father wouldn't let me buy it, but he let my brother get it, and that was all I needed.

For the next couple of years, my brother and I staged Kiss concerts in our bedroom, complete with lights, confetti, and Tupperware containers for drums. I was a fan of all rock music by that time, from Frampton to Foreigner to Styx. They had become my religion.

Then, in the summer of 1978, my brother brought home a new album and said, "You have to listen to this—it's crazy!" He put on song number two, and I sat in amazement waiting for "Eruption" by Van Halen to melt my speakers. It blew our minds, and I decided I had to learn to play guitar.

The only problem was that I was ten years old and didn't have the fortitude to teach myself how to play guitar just yet. So the years went on, and my brother became quite an accomplished guitar player in the Milford High School Jazz Band, while I became a world-class air guitarist—and I'm still pretty damn good at it today! Fortunately, by the time I reached high school, I had managed to teach myself how to play guitar. So had my best friend, Tim Ramos. We were a lot alike. He loved music as much as I did, and he grew up in a music-loving family as well. His brothers all played guitar, and one eventually became a professional musician, playing bass with Blessid Union of Souls. Tim and I wanted to be rock stars, and we lived our lives surrounded by music.

I continued to practice and get better at guitar through college, and I managed to be in a few bands. In the late '90s, I played in a band in Detroit called Bad Juju around the time Kid Rock was playing the bars. However, I was in Detroit to focus on an engineering job, and eventually the band gigs took a backseat to my professional career.

Bad Juju played some of the same bars around town, and we saw his show once. I have to say—I wasn't a big fan at the time, though I love Kid Rock now. He put on a good show, but I didn't connect with his music. In retrospect, who was I to judge? We were just a cover band, and he was writing his own songs. Kid Rock taught me that you have to write your own songs if you want to be the "real deal."

Ultimately, I moved back home to Cincinnati and spent a decade just jamming and doing acoustic gigs with Tim in a band called Mojo Rizin. No, we weren't a Doors cover band, although we loved the Doors. Mojo Rizin was what we had called our swim-team relay group when we were teenagers. We always had to present ourselves with attitude no matter what we did, and the name stayed with us beyond the swim team.

My brother went on to be a Grammy-nominated mixer/engineer/producer for two Incubus records, *Make Yourself* and *Morning View*. Because of our sibling rivalry, his influence never stopped pushing me to be better at music.

By 2008, I was a decent guitarist, and I could play pretty much any song I heard. But after more than twenty years of playing guitar, I had yet to write a single song. I had many bits of music that I had committed to memory, and many more that I had forgotten, but I had never pushed myself to turn them into songs.

Why not? Quite simply because I had no idea how or where to start. Moreover, I was afraid. Afraid I had nothing to say. Afraid no one would like my songs. Afraid *I* wouldn't like my songs. Afraid I couldn't come up with a guitar solo. Afraid I couldn't come up with lyrics that weren't stupid or cheesy. Afraid I would embarrass myself.

Fortunately, with age comes wisdom, and once I reached my forties, I just didn't care anymore what other people thought. Some people are fortunate enough to have this realization early in life. I guess those are the people who become rock stars. However, up to that point, I had been too chicken to take a full-fledged leap into the music business.

But something happened to me one night at one of our acoustic gigs when I was playing the closest thing I had to a song. I was playing the melody on my guitar while Tim was keeping the beat on the congas. A guy I didn't know came up to me and said, "What song was that? It sounded pretty cool!" In that moment, my life changed. It was the reincarnation of me. The new me started believing in myself and what was in my soul. Most importantly, the new me didn't care if other people didn't like my music. It was the first time I had ever played the song for anyone. I knew the song was good, and it only took one person to agree with me to give me validation. At that moment, I realized that I could do this. I could write songs, and I would write songs.

So I went to work. I borrowed my father's MacBook so I could use the GarageBand program to start recording my songs. I came up with a concept for the song "Regrets" that I had riffed in the bar that night. I developed a change and a chorus for the song, and I recorded a basic acoustic track. When I played it back, it blew my mind. I couldn't believe the quality of the recording. *How could it possibly sound this good?* I thought. I had recorded the track by playing acoustic guitar into the built-in microphone of the laptop, and it sounded incredible. I continued to work on the song long into the night, adding a drum track, electric guitar, and lyrics. I was so excited I couldn't go to sleep anyway.

The next morning, after a few hours of sleep, I listened to my recording again, and I was speechless. From that point on, I couldn't stop writing and recording music. I wrote forty-one songs and churned out three CDs in a single calendar year.

Once I had written a song that I loved, songwriting became my focus. I no longer cared about playing cover songs. I had so many new, fresh songs that I really loved. Why would I want to play someone else's songs? I wanted to have the best original band to ever come out of Cincinnati. This is still my mission, and because Cincinnati hasn't produced many famous bands, I still have a chance.

In fact, I didn't even listen to other music for a couple of years. Every day was spent reviewing the latest mix of whatever song I was working on at the time. I only recently stopped playing my music all the time around my kids because I was starting to get worried that they would miss out on all the other great music out there. I needed to expose them to forty years' worth of classic rock, and I wanted to be their guide through the history of rock and roll.

I shared my first demo CD of about ten songs with Jim Murphy, a guy I had recently met who played drums, and another good friend, Tom Pohlman, who was a fellow music lover. They both freaked out about how good the songs were, and I'm not talking about the lighthearted "Yeah, it's pretty good." Jim called to say, "I love these songs. We've got to get a band. When can we jam?" When we finally did get together to jam for the first time, Jim had already learned all nineteen songs I had given him and had put together a set list for the show. He was all in! Tom called me on his drive home from my house to say, "Dude, I can't believe these tunes. I couldn't stop cranking up the volume!" That's when I knew I was onto something. I'm not saying that I'm a great songwriter, but the songs were good enough to rise above the crappy demo tapes these guys had been given by other friends over the years. These two guys didn't have to give me the praise they were bestowing on me. As I passed my music around to other friends and musicians, the praise continued. People were impressed with the quality of the songs I had recorded. And while I may not have let negative comments stop me, the positive feedback I was receiving fueled my passion.

I continued writing, recording, and developing my songwriting style. I slowly established a band of professional musicians, including my buddy Tim. The band is passionate about the songs that I write and we play together. We're now touring and promoting our music. We may never make it, but we're loving the journey, and that's all that matters.

I eventually realized that I had a basic formula for writing good songs. I also learned that not everyone has the skill or will to write a song. Some musicians just can't put it all together. They get stuck like I used to. That's why I'm writing this book. It's not the only formula that works, but it works for me, and hopefully it will work for you. I will do my best to describe the basics as well as the key tricks that I have used to write good songs. The riffs and the song inspiration have to come from you. But hopefully you have some ideas, and you just need a little guidance from someone who has gone through the process of turning a riff into a completed song.

This book lays out truths that I think are important to help you understand how to write good songs from a writer's perspective. It's not about how to create harmony or dissonance or musical fundamentals, because songwriting is much different than musicianship. Each truth covers various guidelines and techniques that you can use to improve your songwriting. So let's get started!

1

The Truth of Rules: There Are No Rules—If It Feels Good, It Is Good

The first truth of songwriting may be the most important: there are no rules when it comes to songwriting. We live in a world of rules, where parents, siblings, teachers, bosses, coaches, managers, and others all tell us what to do. The good news is that music is one of the sacred places where rules don't apply. Music is art, and there are no rules when it comes to art. Oh, people will tell you what they think—what's good, what's bad, and what they like, but it doesn't matter unless you let it matter.

Music, like art, is in the eye of the beholder. If it makes you feel good, it is good—at least for you. You can fart in rhythmic patterns and call it music if you like it. That doesn't mean anyone else will like it, or buy your music, but at least you'll feel good about it!

On a serious note, it's important to define your own songwriting goals. For me it was easy. I love music. It's ingrained in every second of my day. If I'm not listening to music, it's going through my head—literally. It's in my DNA, so to speak, and my brother and father are the same way. The three of us actually hear music playing in our heads when no music is playing. In many cases, it's just some riff or melody I've never heard before. It's a new jam, which I'll ultimately turn into a song if it sticks in my head long enough.

So, first ask yourself why you want to write songs. Is it for fame, for fortune, or to get girls to like you? Maybe it's just because you're sick of playing cover songs. All of these are real reasons for writing songs, so which category do you fall into? Deciding will help you target your craft of songwriting to meet your goals, and it will lead to you being happier with your songwriting experience.

Keep in mind that your goal can be a combination of things that motivate you. If so, you need to keep your goals prioritized so that ultimately you're happy. If your goal is to make money, and you really don't care whether you like the music, you may need to go down a different path than if you want to actually like your music and have your music make you feel good. If you want to just make money, you're in luck, because I'm going to talk about some key techniques to make songs that people will like. But I think the primary goal for writing songs should be to make yourself happy. Once you're happy, then you can worry about your songs making money and creating peace and harmony throughout the world!

Why make yourself happy first? Because the road to making money from your music is long, and there's no guarantee that you'll be successful. In fact, it's very hard to get a song to become a hit. This isn't because a song is necessarily bad but because the music industry and media control who hears new music. They have the connections, distribution, and marketing dollars to ensure that people hear certain music. They get music played on TV shows, on the radio, and in commercials and movies. They decide which songs are "good." In their terms, "good" is what they think will make money, period. Music executives are in the business to make money more than to make good music. This is exemplified in the overproduced, prepackaged, and redundant pop music of today. Industry leaders find a style or recipe that works, and then they duplicate it and make sure that everyone hears it over and over again.

The key is making sure everyone hears a song repetitively. People tend to like any song they hear over and over again because it becomes familiar. As long as a song is in the genre of music they like, people will be more likely to enjoy a song if they have heard it before. When they hear the song again, it is like an old friend that gets better with time.

The Internet has finally made it possible for people like you and me who don't have recording contracts to get our music published, but that doesn't mean our songs will be heard. You can place your songs on social media, iTunes, and every other outlet for people to find, but you still may struggle to get people to listen to and buy your music. Even if your songs are great, if no one hears them, no one will buy them. Ultimately, a song must be heard for it to start making money. This translates to getting lucky in self-promotion on the Internet or getting a record label to promote your music.

Because my priority is to write songs that I love and that make me feel good, I'm happy, and I will die a happy man.

So be true to yourself with your songwriting. If it feels good, it is good! I still sometimes hear or play a song of mine that makes my hair stand up and gives me chills. That is satisfaction for me. It fuels my passion for music and drives me to continue making it.

As a music lover, I naturally like all kinds of music. I believe different music is for different moods. Sometimes I want to rock, and other times I want to chill with acoustic or jazz. I don't have any prejudices against any genre of music. I will listen to any kind of music as long as the songs are good. I know people who don't like certain genres, bands, artists, or songs for silly reasons, such as thinking that type of music is "not cool." I have a friend who hates all '90s rock and roll. He thinks there was no talent in the music, especially in grunge rock. His reasoning is that grunge music isn't as difficult to perform as the guitar playing in the '80s metal era or even the '70s rock era. But people with that kind of attitude toward music are missing out on some great music and missing the point behind "if it feels good, it is good." Music doesn't have to be hard to play or complicated to be good. I love the complex musicianship of bands like Rush, Yes, and Steely Dan, who are all amazing performers and musicians. But where would the world be without simple songs like John Lennon's "Imagine" or "One" by U2?

Throughout this book I say that a good song is a good song, no matter who wrote it, what genre it is in, or who performed it. I even like tunes from Huey Lewis and the News and Cyndi Lauper, who are talented songwriters and musicians even though they may not be thought of as "cool" anymore. The fact that they wrote good songs and made it makes them pretty damn cool in my book.

Cyndi's song "Time After Time" is a perfect example of the cool factor. It's an amazing song, but if I told my band I wanted to play it, they would revolt.

What is cool? People are always going to tell you what is cool and what isn't. Don't be foolish and worry about what other people think. If you're a true artist, you'll love the songs that you create. That should make them cool enough. Naturally, you may like some of your songs better than others, but each song will have its own character or element that makes it cool.

Forget about the critics. I've found that in life, not just in music, the critics are usually people who have failed at whatever they are critiquing. Music critics are usually people who failed at being musicians. Jack Black once said something like, "Those who can, do. Those who can't, teach. And those who can't teach, teach gym." It's funny but true. You have to be your own first critic. Beyond that, you can listen to other musicians and songwriters. But the last word on whether your songs are good comes from you.

Lastly, what you do with a song is up to you. The true essence of that fact is that there are no rules. You can arrange your song in any way you want. You can use any instrument, effect, sample, or style that you like. Feel free to try new things. The songs that break new barriers are usually the ones that get heralded by the critics.

Where would the world of music be if Jimi Hendrix hadn't turned up his Marshall amp so loud that it distorted or Eddie Van Halen hadn't started tapping on his guitar neck to popularize the hammer-on? What if the Beatles hadn't stepped outside the box with the variety of sounds and the use of a symphony on *Sgt. Pepper's Lonely Hearts Club Band?* The only rule is that there are no rules.

Guidelines for Success

There are a million good songs that no one will ever hear. Your song could be next. If you have an idea for a song, don't be afraid to forge ahead with it. Forget what people might think or say. If it makes you feel good, it is good. So focus on what you love first, and it will be a hit, even if only for you. If others like it too, great! And maybe along the way you'll make some money with your song, as well.

1. Do what feels good.
   If you like your song, someone else will probably like it. If not, you have to please yourself first.
2. Experiment.
   Use different sounds, mixing genres or instruments. You could be the first to cross progressive rock or rap with country and create a whole new genre.
3. Focus on the song, not the money.
   Don't focus on money. Focus on making good songs, and the money will follow. If you're serious about making money, take advantage of the following chapters, which present various methods for creating songs that people will understand and like.

2

The Truth of Process: Songwriting Is a Process

The next several chapters can help you leverage techniques that I've learned during forty years of being a music aficionado. The goal is to help you craft songs that not only you but also other people will love. Why do we want others to like our songs? If we love something, we want to share it with others. Getting someone else to like your song gives you affirmation that you're doing something right, and it fuels your passion. Of course, anything worth doing is worth doing for money. If you love your songs, that will be enough. But let's not kid ourselves: you'd love to make money with your songs, as well.

So where do you begin? That is a common question in songwriting. I didn't start writing songs until much later in life because I didn't know where to start. This chapter can help you to get started and to define your process for writing songs.

I'm sure you have heard stories about how songs magically came to famous musicians, such as when Paul McCartney fell out of bed and wrote "Yesterday." It's true that stories like that can happen. Some songs write themselves. But those magical moments are few and far between.

Songwriting is a process, and mastering that process will help you consistently write good songs. Having a process gives you a road map to finishing a song. You may find your own unique process or starting point. But developing your own recipe and defining the steps that work for you will help you navigate and ultimately finish a song. I know a lot of musicians who have bits and pieces of music or ideas for songs, but I know very few who have actually finished writing a song. In fact, being a great musician doesn't always equate to being able to write a song, or more importantly to write a *good* song.

Most of the greatest bands have had one key writer or writing duo that was the driving force. Jimmy Page and Robert Plant of Led Zeppelin, Sting of the Police, Bono and Edge of U2, and of course Lennon and McCartney of the Beatles were the primary writers in their bands. That isn't to say that the other band members weren't important or didn't have input on the songs. Surely the other members contributed to polishing the songs. But typically a principal artist with a vision for the song was the driving force to complete it. In the case of writing duos, one person typically comes up with music, and the other person comes up with lyrics. Elton John writing music and Bernie Taupin writing lyrics collaboratively for most of Elton's songs is a great example of this method.

I always struggled writing songs because I would have a musical bit or chorus lyric but couldn't figure out where to go with it. I had roughly fourteen pieces of music or guitar riffs that I had compiled for more than twenty years, but I didn't know what to do with them. I couldn't just play the same riff over and over for four minutes and call it a song. There had to be some sort of change to complete it.

Eventually, I came up with a chord progression that I really liked. At the beginning of the show or in between songs while we were waiting to play the next song, I would play this partial song as filler music. One night as I was playing this riff, I was struck with inspiration. I was thinking of lyrics to go with the melody, and I started to hear how it could be expanded into a song. I tried a couple of different changes to another chord progression that I had intended to be another part of the song. I tried several different chord sequences until I had something that fit the first progression and made sense. I then started searching for the right chords to take me back to the original chord progression. Before I knew it, I had a song.

What I played that night eventually became the first song I recorded. It is called "Regrets" and made it onto our first album. But finishing that first song took work. I struggled to figure out what I needed to do next to finalize it and fulfill its potential. I used what I learned during the process of making that song to create my steps to songwriting. I break those steps down into these chunks:

- seed
- idea/concept
- core riff/music
- change
- solo/breakdown
- lyrics
- fine tuning

I didn't number these chunks because they can come in any order. However, this order typically works for me. As I said in truth 1, there are no rules. The inspiration for a song can come from anywhere. But when putting together a song, I ultimately think about each of these chunks in different stages to understand what I'm going to do for each part of the song. Oddly enough, a lot of these chunks are developed during recording for me. I often can't force myself to develop a musical change until I get to the point of recording.

Figure 1: Chris Will Songwriting Process

The Seed

The seed can start anywhere in the song. I always hear musical bits playing in my head, some of which are just new jams. They usually come after a night of partying with my friends. The seed could be a musical progression or a riff that I stumbled upon while noodling on my guitar. The seed could also be the concept for a song that comes to me from a conversation, such as talking about my regrets, or a chorus lyric that comes to me out of nowhere. The seed typically becomes the idea or core riff for the song. But every song starts with some seed, and the challenge is to make it grow.

For me, the hardest part of the seed is remembering the seeds. Sadly, I've forgotten tons of ideas over time. This is why it's important to at least get a rough recording of the idea right away. I have rediscovered my ideas years later and turned them into songs, but I wouldn't be writing this book about songwriting had I not turned on my video camera back in 2009 and recorded the fourteen bits of music that I had compiled. That recording led me to start developing the bits of music I had into songs.

When you come up with a riff, press record on your phone or laptop and get a rough recording of the seed so you don't forget it. Not everyone has a recording studio, but you don't need one. I have even used my voice mail and the voice recorder on my iPhone. Typically, I use GarageBand, which comes with Apple computers, to record. Using GarageBand puts me further down the path to finishing a song because the demo is saved while I can continue exploring my ideas. The key is to record the seed quickly. I've found that once I hear another song or piece of music, I lose the seed. If you can't get the seed recorded, at least play it on an acoustic guitar several times to give you a chance at remembering it.

If the seed is a lyric or an idea for a song, I write it down. I used to have a notepad for this, but now I use the notepad in Microsoft Outlook. When I'm inspired by lines in movies or personal interactions, I write the idea or thought immediately. If you don't write your ideas down, you'll forget them.

Then start working your ideas. If nothing else, practice playing the bits that you have. This keeps your tunes prominent in your head and ultimately may lead to the development of other parts. I find it best to work on the ideas when they're fresh because that is when you're most inspired about the idea.

A little over a year ago, my band was preparing to play a big outdoor festival. During the setup of the stage, my drummer nearly cut his thumb off driving a stake into the ground. It was a terrible tragedy that took the band out of commission for about six months. At the time we weren't sure whether his thumb was going to heal or whether his drumming career would be over. We were all pretty sick over the situation.

The following day we were talking about how shocking the incident was and how everything can change in a moment. We were getting ready to play our biggest show of the year, and in a moment everything changed. For all we knew, the band as we knew it was over.

Then it hit me—in a moment, everything can change—what a great idea for a song! As I drove home, I realized that I was humming some music that I thought could have the right tone for this song. By the time I got home, I was singing "Ain't it crazy, in a moment, everything can change." And just like that the song was born. Fortunately I acted on the idea when it came to me. If I had waited around, I might have lost the idea.

In this case, the seed was the idea/concept for the song, but sometimes things can synthesize quickly if you also have a musical seed. I came up with both of these in a matter of hours, but typically my musical and lyrical seeds happen independently.

Conversely, some ideas need time to gel. They may need to sit on the shelf for a month or even years before the right inspiration takes them to the next level. I came up with one of my songs, "Infatuation," in the '80s as more of a metal tune, which fit the musical genre of the time. It took me twenty years to get back to that tune, which ultimately morphed into more of a straight-ahead rock tune than an '80s hair-metal tune. Like fine wine, sometimes songs have to ferment a long time to get the right flavor.

The Idea/Concept

The idea or concept could be the seed for your song or come later in the process of developing your song. Either way will work. The key is not being afraid to explore ideas for songs. I typically start with things that are meaningful to me, such as the painful situations in my life or in the lives of people I know. Other times, I write about things that I think are wrong in the world.

On occasion, I have tried to write about something without a clear idea or concept. For example, I wanted to write a song about my kids, but I didn't know what to write about. So I kept exploring ideas until I came to the concept that we know our kids are going to go through hardships in life that we can't prevent, but we can be there for them. The song became "Someday, I'll Be There for You."

Ideas for songs can also come from the news, religion, a story, or pretty much anything that interests you. The key is to pick an idea or concept that you are passionate about. Passion will show in the song and in your performance of the song. If you believe what you're singing about, others will believe it.

The Core Riff/Music

Like the idea for a song, the core riff/music can often be the seed for a song. This is usually the case for me. I'm a guitar player who grew up in the '70s. I always say I went to the Jimmy Page and Eddie Van Halen school of riffology, because I usually write music the way they did. I come up with a riff while noodling around on the acoustic guitar or the piano. Though most of my songs turn out to be electric guitar-based rock songs, I use acoustic guitar for my noodling because I always have one sitting around.

It is essential to have a core chord progression or riff that is going to define the song. Without it, all you have is poetry, which is okay too. But we're talking about writing songs. It may be another person in your band who comes up with the riffs or music. That is okay as long as someone does it. Along with the idea/concept, the core riff/music will create the seed for your songs. Either can be the starting point for your process.

The Change

For me, the change usually comes when I have the core riff and idea locked down in my head and can repeat it at any time. At this point, I can no longer forget the riff or piece of music, so I know there must be something there that can be turned into a song.

Then the question becomes, where do I go next with the music? I could just play the same riff over and over, but that can make for a pretty boring song. Even so, there are plenty of songs that never change chord progression. For example, "What I Got" by Sublime or "Blurry" by Puddle of Mudd are both pretty much the same chord progression throughout the song. These songs get away with repeating the same chord progression because they employ other techniques such as leveraging the arrangement and layering to achieve a change in the song.

A change is where the music changes direction to create a different part of the song. In most songs, the verse of a song has different music than the chorus. In some songs, a bridge with different music is only played once or twice and is used to connect different parts of the song.

Coming up with the change is almost like coming up with another song. But that piece of music must fit with your riff and make sense so they feel like they're part of the same song. They must come together in a way that makes musical sense. Actually, they don't have to because there are no rules, but if you want other people to like your song, it's a good idea to make the pieces fit together nicely.

I typically try to branch to a new chord progression or riff that is in a key that connects with some portion of my riff. For example, my song "I've Had Enough" has the main riff in A in a progression of A-D-G. The A is used for the intro to the song and the chorus. When it came time to record the song, I had to come up with a different progression for the verses, so I decided to branch off that progression using A-F#-G. This is a similar pattern that starts and ends with the same notes in a different rhythmic pattern.

I wanted to have a small bridge to connect the verse back to the chorus. Using the same methodology, I created another chord progression that utilized at least one of the same chords as the chorus to make it fit together. This isn't the only way of coming up with different parts for songs, but it works for me. Find a starting or ending note in the chorus and use it as a branch-off point to create a different musical part. You will know by how it sounds whether it makes sense for the song.

It diagrams like this:

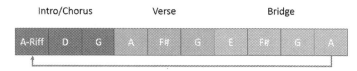

Figure 2: Song Layout

Notice how all three parts incorporate A, which is the key of the song. With this basic idea, if you understand what key your song is in, you can use that key to branch into different directions to create parts for your songs.

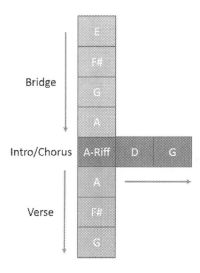

Figure 3: Connecting Chord Progressions

Sometimes, you may only have a single chord progression for a song, but it happens to be a really good chord progression so that the lyrics of the song melodically fit over both. It's possible to use a single chord progression throughout the entire song. You'll hear this method used on a lot of pop songs, but it may be hard to recognize because the song changes the arrangement or the layering between the verse and chorus. This is a perfectly fine approach to writing a song, but you must use some of the techniques I will describe later to change the arrangement or layering.

Once I come up with the different parts, I try putting them together and noodling with them to make sure they work. Once I like what I have, I can paint the vision for the whole song using my basic formula. Through the process of putting together the parts, I sometimes have to swap the music for the verse and chorus because it fits the song better. What I thought was going to be the chorus may turn out to be the verse.

The Solo/Breakdown

The solo or musical breakdown is not required for a song, but it gives the song another place to go. For a long time, I thought the music of the '90s killed the guitar solo. Even though I think the '90s is one of the best musical decades, I wondered for a long time why the solo died. Was it because the music of the time didn't require it? Was it because the art of guitar playing was lost? I don't know the answer, but the lack of guitar solos in music made it a frustrating decade for a guitar player like me.

So I decided I was going to bring back the guitar solo! Maybe my songs haven't become "hits" because it's rare to hear a guitar solo in music these days, and I have guitar solos in most of my songs. For that matter, it's rare to hear rock music in general in mainstream culture. I watched the MTV Video Music Awards recently and I was appalled by the lack of real rock bands. It was bizarre. I thought, *Rock is dead.*

Regardless, I will continue to make rock music, and to me that means having a solo. You may feel differently. If you don't have a solo section, I find it useful to have a breakdown section. This is a section where the song takes a small break to highlight vocals or keyboards. A good example is the middle section of the song "The Old Apartment" by Barenaked Ladies; it could also be considered a bridge.

I typically come up with a guitar solo while I'm recording the song. If I have time and have an idea for the solo, I will go ahead and lay it down while I'm fresh with the song. Other times, I come back after I've had a chance to listen to the basic music for the song several times. Sometimes you need your song to ferment while it is partially finished to allow you to come up with the other parts. Again, do what works for you, which may be different for every song.

The Lyrics

Unfortunately, I can't tell you how to write lyrics for songs or teach you how to be creative. I can only tell you my thought process for writing lyrics.

The lyrics typically come after I'm pretty sure what the music of the song is going to be, including its structure—intro, verse, chorus, bridge, and solo. After I've actually recorded the song and laid out all of the parts, I start to work on the lyrics. At this point I may have an idea for the chorus. Sometimes I have lines I want to use based on the concept or idea of the song.

I typically use Microsoft Word to write the lyrics. First I write down a title that is based on the idea/concept of the song. I have heard the basic recording several times and will start coming up with a melody for the lyrics if I don't already have one. Coming up with the melody and meter for the lyrics can be the difficult part for me. I have found that the best way to come up with one is to hum along with the song and try to lay a melody over the top. No words are even necessary at this point.

If you can't come up with a melody and meter yet, just start writing the lyrics. Your lyrics will naturally want to match the concept or idea of the song. They should serve as little stories. Each may connect with your audience so that the audience understands what you're saying. They should also help build the story behind your concept and lead you up to the chorus, which represents the core idea of the song. Each verse should paint a picture. I also make each line or every other line rhyme. This is standard lyric practice that makes people want to sing along. You can make lyrics that don't rhyme, but rhyming lyrics are easier to remember.

I typically use lyrics over the bridge as the point where I try to create the lead-in to the chorus. It's usually a strong statement in support of the main idea. If I use the bridge multiple times, I repeat the lyrics or some variation of the same lyrics. Repeating the lyrics can help create the hook that makes people sing along. Varying a repeated lyric can help make the song more interesting. I will add more about this and creating the hook later.

For each section of the song, I keep working the lyrics until I am happy. Sometimes that happens very quickly, as some songs just seem to write themselves. Others take much longer. It doesn't matter how long it takes or how many breaks you take from writing the lyrics.

Sometimes I have to change the lyrics during recording to make them fit with the music. When I write, I sometimes try to squeeze too many words in the verse. When I start singing and recording, the lyrics don't fit the melody or meter of the song. This is easily fixed by simplifying and cutting out some words. It's easy to cut out prepositions, which don't really add to the value of the verse. Lyrics don't have to be good grammar; they just have to fit.

In my song "Frienemy," I wanted to say, "I don't like how you're superficial," but it just sounded terrible. So during recording, I changed a word and made the lyric, "I don't like your superficiality," which fit the lyrical meter much better. You may have to invent a new word to make the lyric work with the music.

Naturally, you don't have to wait until you have music to write lyrics. Many of the great writer duos have had a music writer and a lyricist. If you're a lyricist or a poet, it's perfectly logical for you to write lyrics before you have any music. Some writers are true poets who can write a complete song before it ever becomes a song. Remember, there are no rules.

Fine Tuning

The last part of songwriting is the fine tuning of the song. I may modify many elements to polish off the song. Some of these are highlighted in later chapters of this book, so I will speak of them just briefly now.

When it comes to fine tuning, I start with the music and try to see what is missing. Should I add another guitar, strings, keys, or harmonies? I typically add all of these in some form on a song. This is where you start thinking of overlay tracks.

Adding a second guitar part with a little melodic part that goes with the rhythm really gives a song flavor. This is like adding spices to your food. The second guitar should be added sparsely throughout the song. I like to add a second guitar halfway through the verse section or with the chorus to help the song grow sonically. Sometimes the second guitar has different parts that overlay for the verse and chorus. I add keyboards, strings, or piano in a similar fashion. All of these additions help create the sonic wall that makes the song interesting.

I also consider adding in samples and intros to songs at this time. Adding an intro to the song helps give it a signature. Will the song start with just drums, a guitar riff, or a vocal? Your songs should have different intros for variety.

Guidelines for Success

Developing a repeatable process is critical to helping you write songs consistently. Although being a one-hit wonder can be quite profitable for a band like Tommy Tutone with its hit "867-5309 (Jenny)," you probably don't want to create only one song. Here is a recap of the guidelines:

1. Develop a process that works for you.
2. Record your idea before you forget it.
3. Come up with changes to make the song interesting.
4. Make changes branch off the song key.
5. Add solos or breakdowns to give your song a place to go.
6. Add layers to make a full sound.
7. Write lyrics to support your concept.
8. Reuse lyrics to create hooks.
9. Give your song an intro to give it a signature.

3

The Truth of Relevance: People Like What They Can Relate To

People are creatures of habit and gravitate to things that are comfortable and familiar to them. They like to be around people they know, do activities they have done before, and listen to music that seems normal to them. Before people can like your music, they first have to relate to it. Someone who likes country music is unlikely to like your songs if they are heavy metal, as each genre has its own market and fans.

What I'm talking about goes beyond genre. It includes the power of lyrics to connect to an audience. If you're writing instrumental pieces of music, the Truth of Relevance won't apply to you very much. But if you're writing songs with lyrics, it's critical that you write songs that people will relate to. Songs will touch your listener's soul just like they touch yours. Language has the ability to communicate and share the common experiences and feelings of all people. One of the reasons we listen to music is to connect with others on these shared experiences, and because of the way that connection makes us feel.

Lyrics have the power to connect with your listeners in a way that music can't—by delivering on relevance.

Sharing an experience through words that someone else can relate to and know exactly what you're talking about can touch the soul in ways that a musical note can't. It can jar memories of past experiences and inspire a person's hopes and dreams. *Seinfeld* was "the show about nothing," but it was about something. It successfully connected with people because it was about the minute experiences in our daily lives that we all relate to in some way. Seinfeld's observations about daily life were what made the show so great. Your songs need to leverage that same strategy either on an overall topic level or at the lyrical level.

There are many ways to tap into that power. Some of the ways are obvious, and some are not. One of the more obvious ways to connect with a listener is the topic of the song. This should be easy for you to figure out. There are a million songs about having fun, partying, love, war, rock and roll, politics, and I could go on forever. Surely you have an idea you have been trying to turn into a song. The question is whether the idea is a shared experience that someone else will relate to.

Love is the easiest thing to write about, as everybody has been in love with someone or something. But you can't just write about being in love. You must have a new angle to position your song as different and fresh.

I wanted to write a love song about my wife, so I asked myself: What is the indirect angle of that? I thought about all the things I love about her, but I realized it sounded like so many love songs that had already been written. So I started thinking about going in the opposite direction and coming at love from the pain side. This led me to think about the painful parts of being in love with my wife. I remembered when I used to travel a lot for work and how much I couldn't wait to get home to my wife. I would be counting the seconds until I could see her again and looking around corners for her with hopes that she would show up. I thought about all of the fun things we would do when I got back home and how I would fix all our problems. And with those thoughts the idea for "When I Get Back Home to You" was born. I don't use the word love once in the entire song, but it's about love and the longing to be with my soul mate.

Pain is not only an important way to approach songs of love but also the most powerful way of coming at any song to make people connect with your thoughts. In the movie *The Matrix,* an agent makes a point that humans define most of their existence through suffering. Some of the best songs of all time are derived from pain. "You Can't Always Get What You Want," "(I Can't Get No) Satisfaction," and "Layla" are all on the endless list of songs of pain. These songs aren't classified as the blues, although most of rock and roll is based on the blues, but they capture the powerful feeling of pain.

It's been said that "to play the blues, you have to have lived the blues." You have to have endured pain. Maybe you feel like you haven't endured pain, but everyone has endured pain. So search your soul for the things that have been the most painful, and I guarantee you will find a ton of ideas for songs. Jack Black did a great job of encapsulating this concept in the movie *School of Rock* when he asked his students what ticked them off. Their answers were homework, school, and typical examples of preteen angst. He helped them turn their gripes into songs of pain. "I don't want to go to school today, so now

I'm really ticked off!" The lyrics are kind of silly, but the concept applies to whatever you're writing about.

This brings us to the next point—know who your audience is and whom you want to connect with. If it's teenagers, write about stuff they care about, such as school, being in love, and having fun. If it's young adults, you can write about college, going clubbing, or chasing your dreams. If you're writing about the typical experiences of someone in their thirties, you may not connect with high school kids. But this is just a guideline. Plenty of classic songs that kids like are about things they don't understand. A great example is "Lola" by the Kinks. In junior high, I couldn't relate to hooking up with a transvestite, but I liked the song anyway. The guideline is that the connection of shared experience will help a person like your song even more than he or she otherwise would.

Don't limit your songs to being about yourself. You can write about a friend's pain. I have written about my friend's divorce and about other people's stories of being screwed over by someone. Your songs can be a mixture of your experiences and the collective experiences of many. But be aware of a problem that can arise with this. My wife tends to think that my songs are about her even when I'm badmouthing a woman who actually hurt one of my friends. This tells me that I have succeeded in making her connect with the song even if the wrath of the song is really not aimed at her.

Another powerful tool when writing lyrics is to leverage clichés, current lingo, and culture. These act as laser beams of focus to connect with your audience and can also serve as killer hooks, song titles, or even a chorus. Clichés work best because most people use them in their daily language.

A perfect example is "I Heard It Through the Grapevine" by Marvin Gaye. Everyone knows this saying and what it means, so when he wrote this song using this well-known cliché, it became a hit. Other examples include "Great Balls of Fire" and "You Can't Always Get What You Want."

I leveraged clichés for songs like "What Goes Around, Comes Around," "Be Careful What You Wish For," and "I Can't Read Your Mind," which are some of my most popular songs.

Current lingo and culture are also good things to use as song ideas or lyrics for the same reason. People relate to them and probably use them in their everyday language. Famous examples include "What's Going On," "Red Solo Cup," and my song "Frienemy," which is recent lingo for someone who is both a friend and an enemy. Find a cliché, metaphor, or topic to write about and own it.

An even better method is to come up with your own lingo and make it commonplace. Some examples of songs that created lingo or a cliché are "SexyBack," "She's a Bad Mama Jama," "U Can't Touch This," and "I Will Survive." I've heard all of these in common conversations as a result of the song pushing the lingo. That's the power of music. A great song can become part of our mainstream slang.

Lastly, some of the best songs seem simple but have powerful subtexts. These can be the most interesting songs. You don't have to be literal with all of your lyrics. Leave them open for interpretation. Give the audience a chance to try to figure out the meaning or to make it mean whatever they want. This allows people who don't connect with the meaning of your song as you intended to connect with their own meaning. This ultimately widens your audience. Metaphors can be powerful ways to tell stories. Take advantage of the opportunity to be indirect with your lyrics to make it more interesting.

For decades I thought the song "Blackbird" by Paul McCartney was simply about a blackbird, only to find out that the song was about racism and the challenges of African Americans. The song "Panama" by Van Halen is not about the country of Panama but reflects a combination of influences—Van Halen's top fuel car called Panama and a stripper David Lee Roth met in Arizona. The legendary song "Hotel California" by the Eagles has been interpreted by fans in numerous ways. One popular theory is that it is about Satan, but Don Henley swears it isn't. John Lennon once noted that a lot of the Beatles' lyrics were just jumbled words that they put together to fit the music and actually had no meaning at all. Adding some mystery to your lyrics can really increase fans' interest. So get creative with your lyrics, and remember truth 1—there are no rules.

Guidelines for Success

Song lyrics can be whatever you want them to be. They can be crafty, clever, complex, or simple. As long as they make sense to you and work for the song, go with it. Having said that, leverage the tricks that millions of songs before have used to become successful.

1. Create a shared experience.
   Lyrics about common experiences that your audience can relate to will help them connect with your song.
2. Have a new angle.
   Dare to be different. Find a new way to talk about the topic of your song that makes it stand on its own.
3. Leverage your pain.
   Pain is a powerful emotion to tap into, both for finding material to write about and for creating songs with passion that will connect with your audience.
4. Write about everyone.
   Incorporate the stories and experiences of yourself, friends, family, and even people you don't know to help connect with more people. This also helps you avoid people saying that the song is about them specifically, which can make people upset if they don't like the topic. Make your songs about everyone and no one.
5. Know your audience.
   Don't write songs about marriage or losing your job and expect high school kids to connect with it. Understand that only certain demographics of people are going to like a specific song, and that is okay.

6. Leverage clichés and current lingo.

   Clichés and slang are great tools for instantly connecting your song with your audience. If a song title or lyric is something that is commonly said, it's halfway to becoming a hit.

7. Be indirect with your lyrics.

   Find ways to talk about a subject that can be interpreted in many ways. This gives listeners a chance to make up their own minds on what the song is about and create their own mental images and memories for the song.

4

The Truth of Structure: Give Your Songs a Place to Go

Songs can be written in a variety of ways and can take on many different forms. Some can be simple with no changes, such as "What I Got" by Sublime. Others can be complex progressive compositions, such as songs from artists like Rush, Yes, and Genesis. Because there are no rules, all forms can be utilized to create great songs. Progressive songs like "2112" by Rush are almost five songs put together. But when turning a song into something that makes sense to most people, it's helpful to follow some common structural guidelines. Songs need different parts because it gives them a place to go and takes your listener on a memorable journey. If you don't have a well-structured song with different parts, it gets boring very quickly and becomes monotonous.

In this chapter I describe my formula for giving a song structure. It's not the only possible formula, and I didn't invent it. Rather, it's a formula that I derived from a lifelong love of music. Part of the formula came to me naturally. The other part came from studying music that I liked and taking notes on cool techniques that make songs interesting. Though I call it a formula, it's a loose formula that varies using the numerous techniques I will describe later. Varying the structure helps you avoid all of your songs sounding the same.

Structuring a song is pretty straightforward. Almost all songs have a verse and a chorus, which gets repeated multiple times. This can be all you need to create a song. The other optional parts of a song are the bridge, breakdown, solo, and introduction. This is pretty elementary. The hard part, even for the best musicians, is developing an entire song. It's difficult to develop the additional pieces of music to go with the seed riff, which was the idea for the song. I talked about how I use the root key for the song as a branching point to develop changes in "The Truth of Process." Now I will describe how I assemble the parts to create structure for a song and how I create different structures for different songs.

My base formula for structuring songs is the same recipe used by millions of great songs. Every song needs a verse and a chorus. I also like having a solo section because I play guitar and love to solo. But sometimes I include keyboard or piano solos. Most of my songs also have an intro section and an outro section. The intro section is where I give a sample of what the song is about, and the outro section is usually a variation of the chorus.

A diagram of my base formula looks like this:

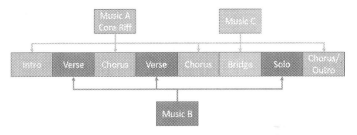

Figure 4: Chris Will Songwriting Formula A

I typically have three pieces of music for a song. These parts are the core riffs that served as the idea for the song. This is labeled Music A Core Riff in figure 4. I typically use this music for the intro and the chorus. The second key piece of music is labeled Music B. I use this for the verse. Typically, I use that verse music for the solo section as well, because the solo comes after the second chorus, and I don't want to use the chorus music back to back. The last piece of music is labeled Music C and is for the bridge section of the song. Good examples of this structure include my song "Lay It on the Line" and "Beat It" by Michael Jackson.

Intro

Looking at the structure of the song, you see that the song starts with an intro that is the core riff. For my base song formula, this is typically the main guitar riff of the song. It could be a keyboard or piano riff too. Classic songs that start with the guitar riff/chorus music as an intro are "Satisfaction" by the Rolling Stones, "Whole Lotta Love" by Led Zeppelin, and "Jamie's Cryin'" by Van Halen.

Another effective intro is to start with the chorus of the song. I once spoke with a record-company executive who verified that this type of intro is often preferred. I also obtained input from radio professionals, who consistently told me that they want to hear lyrics in a song within the first thirty seconds. I guess the days of the long musical intros typically found in classic rock songs are over. If you want to get your songs played on the radio, get to the lyrics quickly. The fastest way to get to the lyrics is to start with the chorus. This method can be found in classic songs such as "If You Could Only See" by Tonic, "Know Your Enemy" by Green Day, and "Any Way You Want It" by Journey.

The intro can also be something that is different from the core music of your song. Examples are as follows:

- sound effects
- drum line
- sample
- count in ("One, two, three, four …")
- musical solo

I've used several sound effects, such as a thunderstorm on "Turn Back Time," ocean waves crashing on "Signs Say You're Leaving," and the sound of a needle on a vinyl record in "Until We Meet Again." Classic examples are birds and a plane on "Goodbye Blue Sky" by Pink Floyd and car horns on "Runnin' with the Devil" by Van Halen. Get creative, try something new, and pick something that ties into the concept of the song.

Using a drum as the intro is also effective, as it gets the beat going immediately and is powerful. It can be done using either the drumbeat of the song or a different drum pattern or solo. Examples are the rhythm pattern in "Lay Your Hands on Me" by Bon Jovi and the drum line in "Walk This Way" by Aerosmith.

Using a sample is a cool way to tie a movie or a famous quote to the concept of your song. One example is a sample of the movie *Cool Hand Luke* in the song "Civil War" by Guns N' Roses.

The count in has been used endlessly in music, but it's still cool and effective. It can be a verbal count in, such as "one, two, three, four," or a drum or guitar click. Using a different language to do the count in can make things interesting. Songs in which the count-in intro is used effectively are "Rock of Ages" by Def Leppard, "I Saw Her Standing There" by the Beatles, and "Back in Black" by AC/DC.

As an intro, the musical solo allows you to show off the talent in the band. Guitar and keyboard solos are the most prevalent in rock history. "Lazy" by Deep Purple is a great example.

Though I typically use the music of the core riff as the chorus for my songs, the core riff may also be the verse of the song. In this case, using the core riff as the intro equates to using the music of the verse for your intro. This has been used in "Waiting on the World to Change" by John Mayer and "In Your Eyes" by Peter Gabriel.

Verse

The verse tells the story of the song in stages. I think of these stages as bite-sized chunks. The bite-sized chunks help transition to the chorus, which typically follows the verse and is the most important part of the song. I usually use two verses per song, and three verses if I have a lot to say. Each verse is at least four lines, which is good for rhyming.

If I have a third verse, I typically put it after a solo, which extends the song and gives the listener one more chance to connect with the lyrics before a final chorus. You can have more than three verses if that's what you need to tell your story.

Each verse should help build upon the story or take you on a journey. The first verse is the start of your story, the second verse is the middle, and naturally the third verse is the end. Another approach is to use each verse as a different example to support the concept. For example, my song "In a Moment" was inspired by my drummer injuring his thumb before a show. But the song ultimately morphed into being about how 9/11 changed people's lives in a moment because I thought it would connect with more people. Each verse describes a different 9/11 story. In verse one, I speak of a man in the World Trade Center before the towers come down. In the second verse, I speak of a wife who telephones her husband before he dies in the towers and a child whose father isn't coming home. In the final verse, I speak of the heroes who gave their lives trying to save the people in the towers. All of their lives changed in a moment.

Find a formula that works and try to write a few songs using it. Then you may try changing the formula using various techniques that I have suggested. Your verses are your canvas, and your possibilities are endless.

Chorus

The chorus is the most important part of the song, and the structure of your song should be focused on getting to the chorus quickly and often. You need to hit your chorus at least three times in the song. You can use it in the middle of the song a few times and then use it at the outro to finish the song with your message. As I mentioned before, you can start the song with your chorus, which can get it in the song for a fourth time. If you repeat the chorus at the end of the song, you can end up pushing the key message of the song ten or more times.

In the first chorus, I keep it short and only sing the chorus once. This enables me to get to verse two quickly. In the second and/or third chorus, I usually repeat the chorus more than once. This enables people to sing along more with the key part of the song. But one key trick is to vary the chorus the second time through. Changing the words makes the chorus more interesting. A good example of this technique is the Tom Petty song "Learning to Fly." Following are the first and second choruses, which are the same. Notice how the third chorus has a slight variation to make the song more interesting.

Chorus 1–2
I'm learning to fly, but I ain't got wings.
Coming down is the hardest thing.
Chorus 3
I'm learning to fly, around the clouds,
But what goes up must come down.

On the outro, I recommend repeating your chorus at least twice and sometimes four times to really get the singalong going. Remember, the chorus is the best vocal part of the song, so repeat it as much as you can.

Bridge

The bridge is optional, but adding one gives your song another layer. This is where your song takes a turn in a slightly different musical direction, which serves to bridge two parts of the song. It can be a special part of the song that delivers a different point of view lyrically, as well. Many times the bridge teaches a lesson learned that ties into the concept of the song. A good example of a bridge is in Don Henley's song "Heart of the Matter":

> There are people in your life who've come and gone.
> They let you down, you know they hurt your pride.
> You better put it all behind you, baby, 'cause life goes on.
> You keep carrying that anger, it will eat you up inside.

Here, Don is trying to tell what he has learned from his experience, but in a different way both lyrically and musically than in the rest of the song.

I typically use the bridge for the same reason and place it in the song to connect the chorus or body of the song to the solo. It creates a nice transition to tell the listener that we've completed the body of the song, and now we're going to jam for a bit.

I sometimes repeat the bridge after the solo, as well, to transition back to the chorus. Other times I use the core riff as a bridge between the chorus and the verse. This works when the riff needs to stand alone or when the words don't fit over the core riff.

Lastly, I sometimes use a bridge to connect the verse and the chorus to create the right musical transition between the two. This allows me to repeat a lyrical hook that prepares the listener for the chorus. "Photograph" by Def Leppard is a good example of this.

Solo

The solo section is a piece of music with an instrumental solo layered on top. It usually comes after the main body of the song.

I typically use music from the verse or chorus, depending on what the solo comes after in the song. If it comes after the bridge, I can use either the verse or chorus music. If the solo comes after the chorus, I use the music of the verse so I don't have two song parts with the same music right next to each other. This provides a change and gives the song a place to go.

The solo can also be another piece of music, as long as it fits with the song. It can lead you back to the chorus, verse, or bridge. A good example of a solo going in a different direction is "Somebody Get Me a Doctor" by Van Halen, where the solo goes to another key. It works because the chord progression ultimately leads back to the same key as the core riff.

Lastly, the solo can be layered over a combination of two key music parts, such as the verse and the bridge. I employ this technique on the song "Another Second Chance." Or you can solo over the verse and chorus music combined, as I do on the song "She Said." Do whatever makes sense for your songs.

Putting It Together

Now that you understand all the parts of a song, here's how you can put them together to deliver good songs that people will understand. Figures 5–7 show several different song structures I have used.

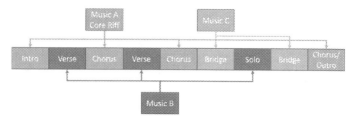

Figure 5: Chris Will Songwriting Formula B

Formula B adds a bridge after the solo to revisit the message of the bridge.

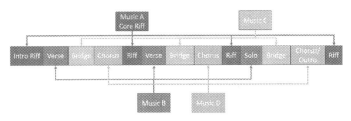

Figure 6: Chris Will Songwriting Formula C

Formula C uses the core riff as a bridge to connect the chorus back to the verse and has a second bridge to connect the verse to the chorus. In this structure, the riff serves as a standalone piece of music that defines the song.

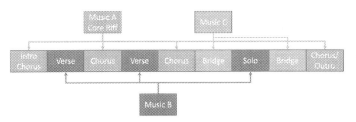

Figure 7: Chris Will Songwriting Formula D

Formula D uses the chorus to start the song, which gets to the lyrics as quickly as possible.

Guidelines for Success

The examples I give in this book are only a sliver of the possibilities, but I have used these four formulas for more than fifty songs. They work, and if you compare them to your favorite songs, you'll find that one of them applies to almost every song that you know and like. Stick to these guidelines.

1. Study your favorite songs.
    Identify the things you like about other songs from a structure standpoint and leverage those techniques for your songs.
2. Develop your formula.
    Come up with a formula that works and that other people connect with.
3. Stick to your formula.
    Once you find something that works, stick with it.
4. Vary your formula.
    Try different variations on your formula to make your songs different.

5

The Truth of Arrangement: A Great Song Is a Great Song No Matter What Instruments You Use

You've probably heard before that a great song is a great song no matter what. This is true. Great songs can be arranged in many different ways with different instruments. Even in different genres, they're still great songs. This is why the Foo Fighters can record a hard-rock song like "Times Like These" and later rerecord it as an acoustic song, and both are great songs. In fact, I would guess that David Grohl wrote this song on acoustic guitar initially and then transferred it to electric guitar. As I mentioned before, I do a lot of writing on acoustic guitar simply because it is easy to grab an acoustic guitar and noodle around in an unplugged fashion.

This is a perfect example of how great songs can be arranged in a variety of ways to capture different moods. The original "Times Like These" is a wall of sound that yields the raw power of Grohl's emotion behind the song. Stripping off the drums, bass, and electric guitars in the acoustic version creates a more somber and soulful sound, but is just as powerful of an arrangement.

So the first step is to write a good song. Assuming that you've mastered the process and know how to structure your song, the next step is understanding how to arrange it. Songs can be arranged in a variety of ways, and the trick is selecting the arrangement that fits the mood you want to present.

When you have an idea for a song, in most cases you also have a vision for the arrangement. You probably already know the genre of the song. But I can't tell you how to arrange the song or what instruments to use. That often depends on what you have at your disposal and what you're capable of playing. What I can tell you is that creating an arrangement that is dynamic can help make the song more interesting.

I like to break song arrangements into a couple of categories:

- stripped
- straight ahead
- epic

Each category has its value, and I believe it's good to create songs from each of these categories to give your song catalog variety.

Stripped

Stripped songs have arrangements that have been cut down to their most basic form to exude the raw passion and inner depths of one's soul. These songs are typically about topics of truth and emotion. They don't need to be dressed up or polished for someone to connect with them.

They're intended to sound simple, as if you were watching the artist perform the song at a coffee shop. These songs form intimate types of engagement with the listener.

Stripped songs have extremely simple arrangements of typically one or two instruments and a vocal. These songs are commonly done with acoustic guitar or piano with one vocal over the top. No extra polish is added because it isn't necessary to capture the desired mood. Great examples of stripped songs are "Going to California" by Led Zeppelin, "Blackbird" by the Beatles, and "She's Got a Way" by Billy Joel.

Straight Ahead

Straight-ahead arrangements are what I consider a typical arrangement. They have drums, bass, guitar, and/or keyboards as a foundation for the core of the song. You don't really need more than this to create a great song, and most great songs use just these instruments. But you can have other instruments if they make sense for your song. An example is a second guitar part that overlays the melody to give it a little extra flavor. Great examples of songs like this are "Hot Blooded" by Foreigner, "Plush" by Stone Temple Pilots, and "Alive" by Pearl Jam.

Epic

Epic songs arrange a barrage of different instruments perfectly to create songs with interesting and extraordinary walls of sound. On top of drums, guitars, bass, and keyboards or piano, an epic song has multiple guitar and keyboard layers, horns, strings, and even samples to give the song a special, memorable signature. Epic songs allow artists to really show their creativity. Great examples of epic songs are "Live and Let Die" by Paul McCartney and Wings, "Us and Them" by Pink Floyd, "Hotel California" by the Eagles, and "Deacon Blues" by Steely Dan.

Building the Arrangement

Each of these song arrangement types has value, though it isn't necessary to classify your songs into these categories. I don't sit around thinking how my songs fit into these categories. I use these categories to exemplify how simple, medium, and complex arrangements can change the presentation of a song.

Once I have an idea for a song, I also have a vision for the arrangement and whether it will be stripped, straight ahead, or epic. Most of my songs are straight-ahead arrangements, but occasionally I come up with a song idea that is special—what I consider epic. For those songs, I try to figure out how I can fulfill that vision.

I usually start by thinking about different guitar parts. I have a second guitar player in my band, and I consider it fun to come up with a second and sometimes a third guitar part. I let the song start with the main guitar, and as the song progresses I add another guitar layer. I usually add the second guitar halfway through the verse, and, if I can come up with a third guitar part that complements it, I add that when the chorus arrives. The adding of layers over time helps build the song to epic proportions.

I also add different instruments, such as strings and synths, to create different textures and accents throughout the song. Adding an organ or piano underneath the mix helps build a fuller sound.

Adding instruments such as the six- and twelve-string acoustic guitar, mandolin, and banjo at the right points in the song can also add some special sauce. Using these additions sparsely rather than throughout the song helps give the song different textures at different times. I also use congas and other percussion instruments to give the rhythm some extra flavor.

Don't forget about vocal harmonies at times in the verse and for the chorus. This helps fill out the arrangement. Nothing catches the human ear like a vocal harmony. I use multilayered harmonies in most of my arrangements simply because people love them. My song "What Have We Done" is a good example of using a multitude of vocal harmonies and instruments for an epic arrangement.

But again, there are no rules. You can do what you like on any song. I find sometimes that a song starts out stripped, and then I add additional instruments to the arrangement because new ideas occur to me as I listen to each new mix of the song. In essence, I let the song ferment, and over time I come up with more ideas. Before I know it, the song has turned into an epic song that I love. The nice part is that I can always strip it back to the bare bones if I want to make an acoustic version.

Just be careful not to put so many layers of instruments on your song that it sounds like a big mess. Don't overdo it. Sometimes less is more. Each instrument must have its place in the mix so that it can be found and have a purpose.

Single Chord Progression Songs

I mentioned earlier that you may only have one chord progression that you want to use for each part of a song. When constructing a song in which the music doesn't change between verse and chorus, you must change the arrangement of the song to make it feel like the music has changed. I use two techniques to make the same chord progression feel different:

• Change the rhythm/picking.
• Change the layers of instruments.

Changing the rhythm/picking of the music in the chord progression is the most effective way of making a chord progression feel different. In fact, utilizing different rhythms is the key to making your songs sound different from one another. I've noticed that some songwriters are stuck on using the same rhythm for everything they write. If you're stuck in this rhythmic rut, you must break free and change up your rhythm patterns. Here are some examples of different rhythms of the same E-A chord progression

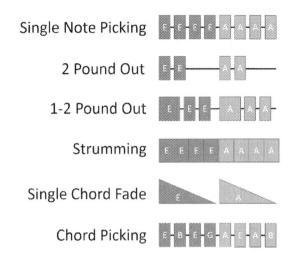

Figure 8: Different Rhythms—Same Progression

For example, if your verse uses basic strumming for a chord progression, try switching in the chorus to what I call a two pound out, which is just two beats of the chord. It looks something like this:

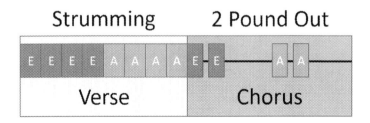

Figure 9: Different Rhythms for Verse and Chorus—Same Progression

Notice that the rhythm of the notes in the chord progression changes, but the progression stays the same. Magically it starts to sound like a musical change.

Single note picking is just picking notes on one string. A one-two pound out is one chord followed by two short chords. A single chord fade is playing one chord and holding it while it fades. Chord picking is just picking through the notes of a chord. These are just a sample of the multitude of variations you can put on a chord progression to make it feel like a different piece of music. This enables you to leverage different rhythms for each part of the song while using the same chord progression throughout. The same philosophy applies to piano or keyboard progressions. "Ain't Talkin' 'Bout Love" by Van Halen is a perfect example of this technique.

The other way to make a chord progression feel different is by adding different instruments. For example, for the verse, use a guitar for the chord progression; when you get to the chorus, add keyboards, strings, and another guitar playing in a different octave or playing a different rhythm while all playing the same chord progression.

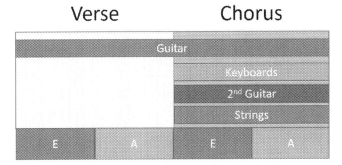

Figure 10: Different Layers for Verse and
Chorus—Same Progression

Using these layers makes the chorus feel like a change has occurred and that different music is being played. That's the goal of this technique: make the music feel changed for each part of the song.

Guidelines for Success

The arrangement of your song needs to be tied to your vision of the song. When you came up with the musical idea for your song, you must have had some vision in your head for what type of song it was going to be. Follow that vision. But don't be afraid to change directions if the song isn't coming together like you thought. Here are some things to keep in mind:

1. Use a variety of arrangements.

Aim to have at least one of each type of arrangement to keep your songs from sounding the same.

2. Experiment.

   Try different instruments and sounds to keep things interesting for yourself and your fans.

3. Let your arrangements build with the song.

   Add instruments throughout the song to help it grow sonically.

4. Align your arrangements with your structure.

   Each change in your song is a great point for adding an instrument to your arrangement.

6

The Truth of Layers: Pull Instruments Off and Put Them Back On

The Truth of Layers is one of the most important truths to understand and master because it keeps your songs from being ordinary. If a song never changes and has the same instruments playing throughout, it can get boring. That's why the masters of production and mixing came up with the strategy decades ago of adding and pulling off layers to make songs interesting.

You've heard this technique in most songs, but you probably never stopped to think about it. These are the parts you really love about songs, and after this chapter I'm sure you'll recognize the layering technique every time you hear it. This layering and pulling off can happen at any part in the song, from intro to outro.

Great examples of this technique can be found in the intros of many great songs, such as "Baba O'Riley" by the Who, "Ain't Talkin' 'Bout Love" by Van Halen, and "Break It Down Again" by Tears for Fears.

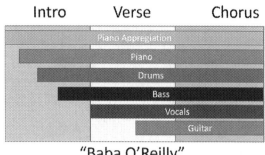

Figure 11: "Baba O'Riley" Intro Layers

Figure 12: "Ain't Talkin' 'Bout Love" Intro Layers

The intro is the best place to start. Most intros employ this technique by default because they start with just one instrument or a partial arrangement of the song. Using just a guitar riff, keyboard line, or drum intro is a great way to start small and build into the full arrangement of the song. Using just one instrument to kick off the song really highlights the signature riff. Building the song as it progresses is the obvious use of layering.

A lot of intros are done with vocals and guitar. I like to use vocals with acoustic guitar for an intro and then let the intro finish by kicking in electric guitar with the rest of the instruments. This gives the song the feeling of kicking into overdrive.

Deconstruction—Pulling Off Layers

A more interesting use of layering is the deconstruction of a song to emphasize certain parts. This can happen throughout the song multiple times and in multiple ways. This gives the song different destinations. It also creates checkpoints in the song for the musicians and listeners.

I typically have the full song kick in to finish the intro to let the listener feel the full power of the song. After the intro, I start the deconstruction by pulling off instruments to emphasize the vocals for the first verse.

One way this can be done is by pulling off everything but the vocal and the bass like I do in my song "Fortune's Fool" or like U2 does in their song "Elevation."

"Fortune's Fool"

Figure 13: "Fortune's Fool," Pulling Off
Layers and Adding Them Back

I start the intro with just guitar and drums and then add vocals and the rest of the instruments. Then, at the beginning of the first verse, I pull off everything except the drums, bass, and vocals, as shown in figure 13 where there are gaps before the guitar and keyboards rejoin the song. This allows the bass line to shine and lets the bassist take center stage when performing live. Another combination that works is to use only vocal and guitar. Then have the bass line kick in halfway through the verse or when the change comes to the bridge or the chorus to let the full power of the song come through. I've also pulled everything off but the vocal and bass and then added piano in the first half of the verse. I then added the guitar to the second half of the verse to create a slow build in the arrangement.

A similar thing can be done in the intro of a song, as well. An example of this is in "Swingtown" by the Steve Miller Band:

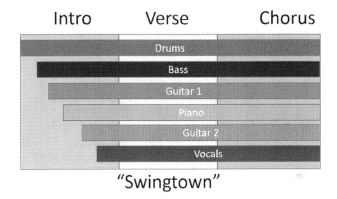

Figure 14: "Swingtown" Intro Layers

I typically don't pull off instruments on the chorus because the chorus is the key part of the song and carries the message. After the first chorus, an instrument can be pulled off for a bar or two to highlight the vocals, and then you can put it back on. You can also pull off everything but the drums and vocals to really highlight the vocals.

I discussed adding instruments throughout the song for just key parts in the last chapter. This is another form of using this technique, but in a more subtle way.

Drum stops are another excellent way to employ this technique. They're typically found at the end of a section, such as the verse or the chorus. Rather than continuing the regular drumbeat or doing a drum roll through the change, you can stop the drum line short or on time with a drum roll to snare stop. This can really highlight the next vocal line. Another approach is to stop the drum line at the change and just keep the kick drum going with the vocals over the top for a bar before you bring all the other instruments back in. This highlights the power of the drums. You can also stop the drums altogether for a bar in the next verse and just have guitar and vocals or percussion such as congas or shakers with the vocals, which keeps the beat going. You can employ drum stops in a multitude of ways with massive effect.

One of the most important uses of pulling off instruments is to pull them off for the final verse after the solo. For some of my songs, I go to a final verse after the solo section. After a big, high-energy solo, it's a great place to bring the song back down to focus on the lyrics. I do this by stripping most of the instruments off and leaving just one instrument to accompany the vocals for the last verse. I used this technique in my song "In a Moment." I pulled off all the instruments except the bass and vocals, and then added piano, and then added the rest of the instruments when the final chorus outro kicked in. This put a spotlight on the bass line and the vocal lyrics. The piano only appears in one place, which adds an interesting effect.

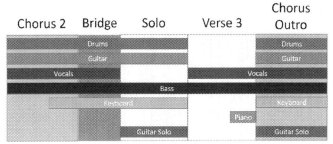

"In A Moment"

Figure 15: "In a Moment," Pulling Off Layers

This deconstructed section can be just an acoustic guitar, electric guitar, bass, or piano. It makes the final verse feel important and is a good time to use your best or most clever lyric. You can slowly add bass, electric guitar, and drums to do a slow climb back to the full arrangement at the end of the verse when the chorus kicks back in. Outside of the intro, this is the most critical place to use this technique.

When you get to the final chorus and outro, put back all the layers to finish the song with full power. I also like to add a second guitar solo or keyboard solo for the outro to take the song to a climax at the finish line.

Once again, there are no rules, but the layering and deconstruction of layers throughout your songs is the icing on the cake.

Guidelines for Success

Layering and deconstructing the layers of your songs is the most important technique to make songs cool. But use layers wisely and differently on each song to ensure variety. Here are some recommendations of my favorite uses of the technique:

1. Pull layers off for the intro.
2. Add all layers to finish the intro.
3. Try vocals and one instrument for the first half of the first verse.
4. Use drum stops at the end of the first verse or first chorus.
5. Bring drums to a stop at the end of the solo.
6. Use just vocals and one instrument on the last verse.
7. Make the last chorus and the outro full power with all instruments.

7

The Truth of the Hook: Make It Memorable

You've probably heard about "the hook" when people are talking about good songs. But what are they talking about? What makes one song have a better hook than another song? I wondered this myself for many years.

The hook is the part of the song that you can't help but love. It can come in the form of music or lyrics and is irresistible and memorable.

I employ the following tools to make a hook:

- a great chorus
- killer riffs
- vocal melody without lyrics
- a repeated lyrical pattern
- vocal harmonies

A Great Chorus

A great chorus is the best hook you can have in a song. The chorus is the most important part of a song, and if you have a great chorus you have the hook you need to have a great song. The best choruses have a great melody and lyrics that touch everyone's soul. Great chorus lyrics can be about meaningful things (think "Imagine" by

John Lennon) or are just fun to sing (like "Happy" by Pharrell Williams). Or they can be naughty, like "Crazy Bitch" by Buckcherry. Some of my favorite songs with great choruses are:

- "Get What You Give"—New Radicals
- "Beautiful Day"—U2
- "Top of the World"—Van Halen
- "The Boys Are Back in Town"—Thin Lizzy
- "We Are the Champions"—Queen
- "Open Up Your Eyes"—Tonic
- "I Got a Feeling"—Black Eyed Peas
- "Who Are You"—the Who
- "Every Morning"—Sugar Ray
- "The Pretender"—Foo Fighters

If you can come up with a great chorus, you're probably going to have a great hook and song.

Killer Riffs

Killer riffs are those amazing signature pieces of music that everyone remembers. As soon as they hear it, they know what song is playing. Great examples of killer riffs have to include:

- "Satisfaction"—the Rolling Stones
- "Ain't Talkin' 'Bout Love"—Van Halen
- "Detroit Rock City"—Kiss
- "Alive"—Pearl Jam
- "Heartbreaker"—Led Zeppelin
- "You Give Love a Bad Name"—Bon Jovi
- "Still of the Night"—Whitesnake
- "Are You Gonna Go My Way"—Lenny Kravitz

- "Lazy"—Deep Purple
- "Cochise"—Audioslave
- "Heroes"—Shinedown

There aren't enough pages in this book to list all of the killer riffs that I would like to mention. Killer riffs create a memory and spark excitement that hooks listeners into the song.

Vocal Melody without Lyrics

A vocal melody without lyrics is when you sing a melody without words. You're simply singing your heart out to a melody that is catchy and interesting. Typically, vocal melodies without lyrics are a surefire way to put the hook in listeners' mouths. It can be as simple as whistling or singing "na na na" or "whoah!" Some of my favorite examples of vocal melodies without lyrics include:

- "Hey Jude"—the Beatles
- "Use Somebody"—Kings of Leon
- "Elevation"—U2
- "Viva La Vida"—Coldplay
- "Young Folks"—Peter Bjorn and John
- "Kickstart My Heart—Motley Crue

Coming up with a vocal melody without lyrics for people to hum along to or sing creates a signature for a song that is memorable and has a strong hook.

Repeated Lyrical Pattern

A repeated lyrical pattern is a technique I use to create a hook in the verse or bridge. My songs "When I Get

Back Home to You" and "Run for Your Life" are good examples of how I apply a repeated lyrical pattern in the bridge of the song.

"When I Get Back Home to You":

All the miles,
All the days,
All alone,
Time's not ticking

All the things,
I didn't say,
All I want,
Time's not ticking away

Notice I repeat the word *all* frequently to make it catchy.

"Run For Your Life":

What you know,
What you say,
Coming for you anyway.

Got your face,
Got your name,
Gonna find you anyway.

Notice how I repeat the words *what* and *got* to drive the lyrics of the bridge. Repeating the first word of the first two lines of each of these bridges makes them catchy and creates a strong hook, especially when combined with two pound-out rhythms for the guitars.

Harmonies

Vocal harmonies are the most powerful thing in music. I love all kinds of music, and love a well-crafted composition, but vocal harmonies rise above everything else for me. When I see bands playing live, vocal harmonies are always the thing I notice that sets great bands apart. It's important to work hard putting killer harmonies in your songs. Killer harmonies create a hook for any listener. Some examples of my favorite songs with amazing vocal harmonies are:

- "Because"—the Beatles
- "Seven Bridges Road"—the Eagles
- "Bohemian Rhapsody"—Queen
- "It's Love"—Kings X
- "Peg"—Steely Dan
- "Last Plane Out"—Toy Matinee

It's hard to achieve vocal harmonies at the level of these songs, but if you can achieve a three-part harmony in your song, it will be a strong hook.

Guidelines for Success

You don't have to have a hook in your song, but without it, it's hard to make your song memorable and make it a hit. Here is a recap of the key techniques I recommend using to create a hook:

1. Put the hook at the beginning of the song.
   If you have a great riff or chorus, there's no sense in waiting around to hear it.
2. Use vocal melodies without lyrics.

Get people dreaming about your songs with something they can't help but sing or hum along with.

3. Get a unique riff.

   Make your song more than just a chord progression. Give your song its own signature.

4. Use harmonies whenever possible.

   Layer the chorus with multilayered harmonies to make it amazing.

5. Use repeating lyrical patterns to make lyrics memorable.

   Lyrical patterns are simply easier to remember, and you want people to remember your song.

8

The Truth of Simplicity: Less Is More

I grew up listening to all kinds of bands, and Rush and Yes were two of my favorites for a long time. Their style of rock was known as progressive rock because it was complicated and showed off how talented they were as musicians. They had songs that lasted an entire album side—truly epic. For a long time I thought they wrote the greatest songs because they were the hardest to play and the most intricate; therefore, they had to be the best.

But the greatness of a song isn't about how complicated it is or how difficult it is to play, though there is merit in both of these attributes. It's worthy to appreciate the musicianship of bands and their amazingly epic songs. But I learned as I got older that there is beauty in simplicity. Greatness can be found in how pure and simple a song is. This changed my whole outlook on music.

I still love Rush and Yes, and I appreciate their music as much as I always did. I also still love to play difficult pieces of music. Playing challenging music helps improve us as musicians. But I no longer feel the need to write intricate or complicated music like I used to. In fact, this desire to write and play progressive music in the belief that I might become a heralded musician is actually what held me back and kept me from writing music for many years. I guess writing progressive rock music isn't what flows in my veins. At least it isn't the kind of music that comes to me out of nowhere. I still love that type of music, though I don't listen to it much anymore. But I rarely get that type of song idea to pop inside my head or come out of my noodling on the guitar. So why would I write that kind of music?

Fortunately, my core taste changed, and I discovered that I really liked straight-ahead rock over progressive music. I started loving simpler songs because they were more fun to listen to and great for partying. This opened the door for me to write my own music. Because inspiration comes from within for me, my songs are usually the result of simpler straight-ahead rock jams. That is what works for me.

Now that I realize my strength is with straight-ahead rock jams, I don't waste time thinking about writing progressive music. You should stick to your own strength, whether it is progressive rock, country, or another type of music. As I learned, whatever type of music is coming to your head is most likely what you should be writing.

I know bands and musicians who spend a lot of time trying to write complicated pieces of music. Maybe they write straight-ahead rock or metal songs but spend too much time trying to make them hard to play. For example, they try to create complicated chord progressions and have guitar solos that are blazing fast with complicated runs. Maybe they do this because that is what comes to their heads, but I think that they think it will make them appear to be better musicians. The problem is that their songs aren't very good. Much of the original music I've listened to locally sounds like the band spent too much time focusing on complicated music and not enough time writing good songs. If the songs are good, the complicated runs and solos will be good, too. And once a good simple song is created, complicated runs can be added. But it's definitely more challenging to write an intricate song that is also good. The quality of the song isn't everything; it's the only thing. Making a song that makes sense to others will make it likeable. If you want your song to make sense, break it down to its simplest form and see if it is still good. Pull out your acoustic guitar and do an acoustic version—a stripped version, so to speak. If it is a good song stripped down, it will be good with all the extra flavor on it. If a song doesn't sound very good as a stripped-down version, it probably won't sound better when you make it complicated. As the saying goes, "You can't perfume the pig." Just like a good song is a good song no matter how you arrange the instruments, a bad song is a bad song. This is why good rock songs are still good rock songs when bands do the "unplugged" version. The acoustic version is like a litmus test.

So, when you write, think about the earlier chapters dealing with process, structure, arrangement, and relevance to make sure you focus on creating a good core to the song in its simplest form. Then you can add flair and layers if you still want to make a complicated song. Like I said before, progressive rock is awesome, but make sure the foundation of the song is good first. Sometimes I come up with more complicated things, as well. If a tune comes to my head and sticks there for a while, it's probably going to be good because I can't forget it. This is a good guideline: If a melody comes to your head and you can't get it out of your head, it's probably going to be good. If it's from your soul, it's going to be good.

Guidelines for Success

Keeping it simple isn't hard to do. Some writers just overlook this guideline. If you keep this in mind while writing, it will pay off.

1. Test your songs stripped down by playing them acoustically.
2. Focus on good songs and what is in your head.
3. Don't try for complexity.
4. If it sticks in your head, it will be good.

9

The Truth of Originality: Inspiration Comes from Many Directions

One of the things that can worry writers, including me, is writing songs that are original and don't sound like something else. Though this is an important thing to think about, you also have to keep it in perspective. Remember, there are only twelve notes to work with in music. Though they can be arranged in a multitude of ways, the number of combinations is finite.

It's almost a certainty that one or all of your songs is going to have some element that sounds like another song. For starters, most bands are working from the same palette of instruments. The drums, guitars, pianos, amps, vocals, and keyboards of today still sound like the instruments of the past. In fact, most musicians are always out looking for vintage gear because they love the tone vintage gear produces. So why wouldn't your songs have elements that sound like other songs? Production quality has drastically improved, and digital recording has made it possible for anybody to record great-sounding music. But in general, rock still sounds like rock, and country still sounds like country. There is no changing that, and that is more than okay—it's great. We all have a lexicon of music that we love from our past that inspires us to write our own songs. So roll with it, and don't worry about whether various elements in your music remind you of other songs. However, do be cognizant of your music to make sure it doesn't sound *too* similar to another song.

There are always going to be some people who criticize your songs. Your naysayers could say that your song is a rip-off of some other song. Don't pay attention to those people—unless it really is a rip-off. But if it's not a rip-off in your mind, be prepared to defend your song. Know what is different about it while acknowledging any similarities that exist.

Once, a friend said that one of my songs sounded like another popular song. My song was in a different key, had different parts and chord progressions, and had different lyrics and theme. Once I pointed these things out to my friend, he realized that my song was very different from the other song. The average listener may not know about music keys and progressions. This person might peg the overall sound or tone of the song as similar to another song and might not be able to identify the musical elements that are different. The key is that you should be able to identify the differences when challenged.

Inspiration can come from anywhere. The Beatles were inspired by Chuck Berry and Buck Owens. Led Zeppelin was inspired by many of the great blues artists. In fact, Led Zeppelin borrowed so much from Willie Dixon's old songs that they had to give him credit on some of their songs on the first album. But the influence of these artists is felt on many songs where they may have borrowed ideas or bits and made their own musical offshoot. They took these bits and combined them with

Celtic acoustic sounds, and many more bits and pieces mixed with their own music to create their own style.

If you got too critical, you could say that 99 percent of blues songs are a rip-off of some other song. Blues songs all follow the same pattern, and thousands of blues songs are almost exactly the same except for the lyrics. But that doesn't stop people from loving the blues or guitar greats such as Stevie Ray Vaughn, who took the blues and then shredded it with his molten guitar playing. But his songs are still the blues, and many of them are just like other blues songs. This is what I call being inspired.

David Lee Roth said something like, "If you steal from one person, it's plagiarism. If you steal from everyone, it's inspired." He's right. Your influences in life and in music are what make you who you are and make your music what it is. So borrowing bits and pieces, ideas, or techniques is only natural, and in many cases it's subliminal. Your musical style probably has elements of all your favorite music. You may love the way someone plays guitar or the way a singer does a particular vocal on a song that you love. It's perfectly okay to pick up these styles and make them your own.

Eddie Van Halen is my guitar hero, but if you listen to my songs, you wouldn't say that they sound like Van Halen or even like Eddie himself. That's because my guitar style and songwriting style are a blend of much more than just the style of Eddie Van Halen. There are bits of Jimmy Page, Steve Howe, Alex Lifeson, Angus Young, Chris Robinson, Tony Iommi, Randy Rhoads, Warren DeMartini, George Lynch, Joe Walsh, and so many more. If I think of my songwriting, it is the same—Van Halen, Led Zeppelin, the Doobie Brothers, Kiss, the Black Crowes, Tonic, Stone Temple Pilots, ZZ Top, and even a little Beatles, all blended together with my own special sauce.

Decades ago, rap artists started taking samples of other songs and building their own songs off of them. Many people said they were stealing. Today that practice is so mainstream that the law has changed. Now you're allowed to sample small parts of songs to incorporate in your songs. In the digital age, sampling will only continue to grow. As long as you take the sampled bit and do something new and fresh with it, I say go for it. If you're looking to take an entire song and do a cover of it, or take the music of an entire song and make something new from it, make sure you get a license to do it, or it will be copyright infringement. For example, Kid Rock's "All Summer Long" is a blend of "Sweet Home Alabama" by Lynyrd Skynyrd and "Werewolves of London" by Warren Zevon. To make this song, Kid Rock had to get permission from the copyright holders for these songs, and he probably pays them a royalty.

You can now pay to license a song to make a cover or do a sample much more easily than in the good old days when you had to get direct permission from the rights holder. Online companies provide this as a service.

So don't be afraid to be inspired by other bands, songs, or sounds that you hear. That is what the record industry does. It finds something that sells, and then it duplicates the formula over and over again with multiple bands. In the 2000s, there was a flurry of bands that sounded like Nickelback and the Dave Matthews Band. Record companies were signing similar bands because the recipe worked and because they knew they could sell more music replicating the same kind of music. That's why songs start to sound the same. I've heard recent pop songs that were almost identical in chord progression and style but with different lyrics and arrangements.

The mix of all your influences may create the next great sound, which will be yours. Originality probably comes naturally if you're a true artist, so create something new even if it is built on elements from the past.

Guidelines for Success

Musicians of today are standing on the shoulders of giants. We missed out on the birth of rock and roll, but we can learn from the past to make new sounds and sometimes better music.

1. Don't steal—this is obvious.
2. Be inspired; leverage your influences.
3. Build on ideas from everywhere.
4. Blend ideas; stir the music melting pot.
5. Be aware of the elements of your songs that sound like other songs, and try to avoid it.

10

The Truth of the Mix: A Good Mix Is the Difference between Being Heard and Being Lost

The last truth of songwriting is actually less about songwriting and more about the importance of a good mix and mastering for your music. I want to briefly cover this topic because I have learned a lot since I started writing and recording my songs. I want to share my experiences so you can learn from them.

When I first started recording my songs, I was blown away by how good they sounded. I couldn't believe that I could put together songs in GarageBand that sounded so great. The truth is, in comparison to a fully produced song you hear on the radio, they didn't sound very good. They sounded like demos. Maybe they were better than the demos my friends used to give me on cassette tapes, but they still didn't have the dynamic range comparable to songs you hear on the radio, or even most classic rock songs from the 1970s or '80s.

I had no experience in mixing or recording, so naturally I couldn't make the songs sound like I wanted them to sound. I just didn't know all the tricks of the trade.

At the time I didn't care. I figured that any real artist, musician, or music executive who heard my songs would look past the quality of the recording and mix. I was wrong.

I shared my songs with an awesome musician friend of mine. I checked back a few weeks later to see what he thought, and his response was lackluster. All he could say was that the mix wasn't very good, the dynamic range of the recording was poor, and other elements of the sound weren't up to par. About two years later, I went back to him after I had learned a lot about mixing and producing by trial and error. By this time, the quality of my mixes was tremendously better—actually radio quality. He listened to the exact same songs and was blown away. When I told him that the songs he was hearing were the same songs he had listened to two years before, he couldn't believe me.

The point is that many people, even great musicians and people in the music industry, can't hear through a bad mix to judge a good song. This isn't surprising, because most people also can't write a good song. Some people do know a good song when they hear it, but unfortunately that usually requires a completely finished product.

I sent my songs to another friend who is a mixer/producer/engineer and basically got the same kind of reaction. "You'll want to fix the drum sound," he said. I'm not upset with my buddies for their reactions—they were just telling me the truth. The songs weren't ready for primetime. But that isn't what I was looking for from them. I was just looking for them to say the songs were good. But some people can't get past the mix, or maybe they just don't have time to. I had other friends who could hear past the mix quality, which was refreshing.

I also sent my songs to a friend in the song-licensing business who promotes songs for TV and movies. When I sent her my first batch of songs, her immediate reaction was that I shouldn't send her my songs until they were mastered. Her rejection had nothing to do with whether she liked my songs. She just couldn't advance them in her industry unless they were fully produced. That's how the music business operates. People in the business want finished tracks that are ready to go. My belief was that I could pitch my songs and hear, "The mix needs work but the songs are good. Let's get you in the studio." That was just a fantasy that I saw in the movies, I guess.

In the age of the Internet, your songs have to be ready to go before anyone will even listen to them. Even then people may not listen to them. People in the music business don't care about your music unless they think they can make money from it. You have to adopt the style of another big current band, be young, and have "the look" to get the music industry interested in you. Forget about song quality. That can be written for you, too. Plenty of writers can churn out songs for bands that meet the other criteria the industry needs to sell music and make money. If you are just interested in writing and licensing your songs, this could be a good outlet for your songwriting.

The only other way to get people in the business interested is if you start getting a ton of hits on YouTube or actually start making big money selling your music yourself. If you pack venues with people coming to see you perform your own music (not cover tunes), you will generate interest. Once you start selling your music on a big scale and packing clubs without the industry's help, people in the business will come knocking like the mafia because they want a cut. At that point you'll have become an opportunity for them to make more money, which is no different than any other business in the world. If business executives see something new that works, they try to snatch it up and grow that business rather than recreate it themselves.

So how did I learn to mix? I learned the old-fashioned way: repeated tries. I mixed songs over and over every night into the wee hours of the morning. I tried different things each time. I also spent a lot of time listening to other songs that I liked and taking notes on their mixes. Ultimately, I learned some key things about mixing that really help. Here are my key tricks:

- Record everything with a direct line.
  When I first started recording, I was recording into the laptop condenser microphone that is built into the MacBook. This cuts down your dynamic range. Make sure your guitars, keyboards, bass, acoustic guitars, and vocals are plugged directly into the computer. This gives you a full sound and dynamic range. You need some sort of USB audio interface to do this. I bought a PreSonus USB interface for about $150, and it works great.
- Get a good condenser vocal studio mic.

A good mic really helps your vocals sound crisp. I bought a Rhode Studio mic for about $400. If you can't afford that, use a Shure SM-58.

- Pan your mix.

  The point of a mix is to give each instrument a spot that makes it easily audible to keep your music from sounding like mud. So make sure you pan things in different spots. For example, I usually have drum snare and kick, main vocal, and keyboards, which are typically stereo, in the center of the mix. Then I pan guitars to either side, along with other instruments and other vocals.

- Double your guitar track and pan left and right with them shifted slightly.

  If you're making rock songs, double the main guitar track by taking the original and copying it onto a new track. Then offset it or delay it 0.036 seconds so it's slightly behind the original track when you play it. Then pan the original to the left and the copy to the right. This makes your guitar sound massive and full, like two guitars playing the exact same thing. This takes advantage of your left and right speakers fully, so that your left and right ears get a fuller sound. This is an important and amazing trick.

- Get an analog compressor.

  This is a tip I got from my brother. He told me about an analog compressor software plug-in called "The Glue" that works with GarageBand and that emulates the old SSL or Neve analog mixing boards of the 1970s, which are known for their warm sound. This will warm up your mix and make it phatter!

- Make bass and drums loud.

  Make your drums and bass louder than everything else in the mix. This gives the beat of your song a solid foundation. Because they are low-end instruments, they won't drown out your guitars and vocals.

- Master your songs loud.

  In today's music market, songs are much louder than when I was young. To get your songs played on the radio, they have to be as loud as everything else on the radio. So turn it up. I usually turn my master volume on my mix almost up to peaking such that it touches the red on the meter with every beat.

Guidelines for Success

Your songs must sound good if you want someone to even think about listening to them. Once you've completed a song, start working on getting a good mix, and keep tweaking the mix until you get it right. It might take some time to learn how to do this, but it will be a fun journey.

1. Get a MacBook and audio interface.
2. Listen to and study other songs' mixes.
3. Work hard trying to get people to listen.

11

The Final Analysis

Songwriting isn't easy; if it were, everyone would be doing it. You may find out that you too can't write songs—I don't know. But there's only one way to find out, and not getting started because you don't know where to start would be a shame. If you love music like I do, and you really want to write music, I've just given you some simple guidelines to help you get started.

You might find that you can write good songs, and songwriting will become your biggest hobby, if it isn't already. I have had many successes in my life and in business, but my greatest joy, outside of my family, is making my own music. Some of my proudest moments are hearing my songs—it still makes my hair stand up.

So get started. What are you waiting for?

Printed in the United States
By Bookmasters